# Things I Hope No One Will See

Payton Ray

BookLeaf
Publishing

India | USA | UK

Presentation by *BookLeaf Publishing*

Web: www.bookleafpub.com

E-mail: info@bookleafpub.com


ISBN: 9789358319811

First edition 2024

# It's The Little Things

There is something about the way
your eyes shine brighter when you smile
that makes me want to tell nonsense jokes
forever
just to hear you laugh.

# Bliss

His lips entice me
like the waves intrigue the moon
and the trees attract the birds.

His eyes
light emeralds in a dark cave
never fail to paralyze me
with each look.

I want to taste his lips and
hold his heart.
I crave to touch him and
dance with his soul.

Like the wind helps plant beauty
all over the world
I want him to take me with him
wherever he goes.

# You Are My Biggest Muse

I want to write music as illuminating as your eyes.

I want to compose rhythms as intoxicating as your personality.

I want to create magic

art

compositions

stories

all as momentous

alluring

and innocent as you are.

# Twin Flame

Maybe I need you so I can heal you.

I'm maternal, I know.

I'm protective.

I get concerned.

I want to help you

even when I know I can't,

even when I know I can't change you.

Maybe I never give up because I know

you're worth it,

because I know who you are inside,

hidden from the world,

hidden from yourself.

You're just like me.

# Send Me to AA

5

I can't stop looking at you.
Your presence is
intoxicating.
You make me feel
drunk, and
I never want to be
sober again.

# You Are a Gardener Too

Your only fault is
your inability to see beauty where
it is planted,
starting at your own feet.

# Sometimes My Anxiety Sucks

A rope pulls, yanks, tightens around my neck,
wrenching out every last breath,
I try to rake the threads apart,
but my nails are not very sharp,
my fingers only glide across,
boiling hot from the friction,
"just be happy" they scoff,
I think, "what a conniption"

# I'm Not Ready to Be a Mom

There might not be a name for it,
at least not one that will do it justice,
this magnetic pull,
this wave of longing
and wondering
and wanting.
This is something I need.

It has devoured me since I was little,
chewed me up,
swallowed me whole.
Maybe I'm still stuck there
in that place where I can touch my dreams.

# Just Another Girl On the News

Love is illogical.
It blinds you.
It captures you.
It reels you in and keeps you warm and
assures you those pants do not make you look
fat.
And then it raises its voice and
holds your head underwater and
snickers to the slowing beat of your heart
as you take your last breath.

# Foundry

The words you said to me still burn
the insides of my brain,
the flames licking at the memories,
lapping at my thoughts,
leaving nothing but a crisp powdery reminder
of how much I have lost.

Nothing can douse me now.

# Clipped

There is a numbness in my chest that
constricts my airflow.
Breathing has become a chore.
The drunk fluttery feeling that you left
behind is gone now.
I'm afraid I will never fly again.

# Storm Warning

There is a rumbling in my soul that won't go
away.
Every time you come close
the stitches of my old wounds break open.
My fingers ache with a longing to touch you.

If I was logical
I would walk away
But I've never been one to listen with my head
over my heart
or to juggle the storm that is brewing inside of
me.
Lock the windows and
head downstairs
because
it will not hold back.

# The First Day I Didn't Cry

13

When I am away from you
the clouds in my head evaporate
and the skies clear.
The sun beams so bright through the freezing
air that I have to squint my eyes just to see
that I can in fact still breathe
without you.

I never thought I was capable.

Today I discovered I am invincible.

# Torture

Because of her torture I cannot eat
I am crushed by the feelings of being alone
I am drowning in feelings of defeat

There is never a day where I can cheat
For it is an old mistake I have always known
Because of her torture I cannot eat

She brings along her friend for me to meet
With balding stale hair and eyes cold as stone
I am drowning in feelings of defeat

It's quite discomforting the way she greets
You, flaunting all her skin and bone
Because of her torture I cannot eat

Step on the treadmill and move your feet
Work every day to get that number down
I am drowning in feelings of defeat

My body is not mine, this war I cannot beat
I am a stranger in my own house and town
Because of her torture I cannot eat
And still I drown in feelings of defeat

# Friends That Can Pick Up
# Where You Left Off

She is there

She is there at night

That voice in your head

That makes it hard to sleep

That brings up bad memories

That makes you reflect on your mistakes.


She is there during the day

That reflection off the window

That title on a magazine cover

That voice on the radio

Advertising weight loss programs

and plastic surgery.

She is that edge in your mother's voice

When you ask her how you look

When you ask for seconds at dinner

When she sees you reaching for dessert.

She is that scoff from your dad

When he sees you wearing skin-tight clothes

With a body like yours.


She is there

She is everywhere

In every voice that is spoken

In every sentence

In every song and book and story

In everyone you know.

She rules your world.

She is there.

# Why Am I Like This?

I listen to the sound of my stomach
begging and crying,
but I do not reply.

When my bones protrude and show
bright as day
and clear as crystal
I can't keep my fingers off
myself.

I am not myself anymore.
But I do not know who I am now.

Before,

I never desired such things.

Things like hip bones
and collar bones
and wrist bones
and thigh gaps
and ribs on my stomach.

I used to think those things were
dangerous signs.

Now I pray at night
for such things,
and I torture myself
just to become them.

# Total Body Makeover

Like ripples in a pond
or waves in the ocean.
Like divots in the sand
and tips of mountains
As sharp as carved spears,
admired like fine china

There is no cushion left
to seat us
There is only the need to
be like sheets
Transparent and light
everything in between

Collars flaunting pools
to fill up with your treats
Because we don't need them

We have our own way
to feel alive

# Nothing But Air, Love Ana

Listen close now challenge yourself work hard
and never give up you're not seeing results? well
Rome wasn't built in a day now was it? eat less
eat only fruits and veggies don't eat after six pm
it all sits in your stomach and turns into fat your
mother is right you need to lose weight you need
to walk around the track at the YMCA you need
to do situps and pushups and stretch so run every
day run after band practice run before marching
band performances run at night do jumping jacks
downstairs at two in the morning so no one will
hear you and no one will suspect you hide food
in your sleeves feed it to the dog throw it in the
trash can flush it down the toilet give it away to
people so you don't shove it in your fat fucking
mouth get rid of all your bigger clothes so you
don't have a backup plan if you gain weight
because you won't don't allow yourself to do so
don't eat don't eat don't eat "But I haven't eaten
in 3 days!" good that is what you have to do
don't crumble under the pressure don't give in to
the pain and the exhaustion you have to believe
that nothing tastes better than skinny take baths
in freezing water it burns calories you need to
burn calories if you consume more than you

burn off you will get fat if you eat that cupcake
you will get fat if you let yourself binge today
you will get fat if you eat that hotdog you will
get fat don't go to lunch skip lunch stay in the
band room distract yourself from your hunger
your stomach growling is good it is the cheering
and applause of a job well done don't listen to
your friends they don't know what's good for
you ignore them push them away don't let them
in don't tell anyone about me don't confess to
your mom she will not believe you no one will
believe you because you still look like a
disgusting overweight whale only I can help you
let me help you let me give you what you've
wanted for years step on the scale every morning
and every afternoon and every evening and
every night four times a day five times a day
keep count keep count of your calorie intake
keep count of the amount of reps you do during
your workout keep count of how many days it
has been since you last ate write to me write to
me about your feelings write about how proud
you are write about how much you wat to thank
me write about how hard you will work with me
to achieve your goals let me help you let me
guide you let me show you how to shrink
yourself down to nothing tell yourself that
skinny is everything believe in me believe that
starving is the only way to be perfect discipline

yourself don't eat that! put it down! great now you know what you have to do run into the bathroom stall slide the lock and get on your knees bend over you know what's next far far far down shove that finger far down your throat let all the food come up let all the guilt and calories and shame empty into the toilet bowl and feel embarrassed feel pitiful feel horrible for eating that you know better steal your sister's medicine take those laxatives several times a day even when you haven't eaten mix them with water only because water has zero calories drink and swallow and keep it down so you can cleanse your fat ass stomach and finally be free and pretty and then give yourself the willpower to help yourself lie if you have to lie to your friends like to your family and teachers and loved ones and doctors manipulate them you see that body in the mirror? that's what you look like you think it can't be true that the number on the scale doesn't match your reflection but trust me you are still fat you are still gigantic an obese and heavy and monstrous but I can help you put your trust in me let me show you the ways so soon enough you will be nothing but air let me set you free let's make them regret the day they dared to call you fat.

# I Only See You as a Friend

Like a plague I avoided you.
Every long way round,
every detour that made me late,
it was all worth it.
To not have to stand in the same dungeon that
you transformed work into,
to not have to tremble under the sweltering
pressure of
your eyes
transfixed on the body you helped yourself to
while I rested comatose from liquor
in the bed of your best friend's son,
to not have to clench my chest with quivering
hands
as I plod past the beckoning windows
so impatient to replay the suffering that occurred
there.
I'd drive and run and walk and dance through
every
hidden in and out of town
inhaling the present,
exhaling the past,
dreaming of the day the
sound of your name
won't make me
quake.

# You Bring Out the Survivor
# in Me

You bring out the survivor in me,

the brave soul who can wear tight jeans again

and low cut tops,

who can finally look at the outfit she wore that
night
and honestly believe she doesn't need to burn it,

because there was never a correlation

between her clothes

and your actions,

who isn't afraid to go to the places she used to
love

even if there's a chance you might be there

and even if she knows you will.

You bring out the survivor in me,

the hockey-loving

personal cheerleader

free-spirited girl in me,

supporting her brothers again at the rink

because she can finally see your face again,

the girl who crammed all her feelings inside

a tiny glass bottle

and watched in horror as they simmered

and popped

and bubbled,

overflowing at the top

and oozed down over her self-control

and her confidence,

drowning her,

the girl who became afraid to smile,

to make eye contact with any boy,

any stranger,

the girl who collapsed in on herself.


You bring out the survivor in me,

the girl who was afraid to get close to another
guy,

who got nervous when he touched her,

and scared when he tried to kiss her,

who couldn't trust the boy who now loves her

and praises the ground she walks on.


You bring out the survivor in me,

the girl who fought herself to go back,

back to where it all happened,

who choked on tears as she told her closest
friend,

the girl who chased you down in the hallway

furious, steaming mad

betrayal scarred across her face

like red streaks from a blazing fire,

the sparks crackled across her skin,

the girl who stopped you in your tracks

and demanded that you admit what you did.

The girl

who was told

"I don't remember any of that."

The girl who sobbed in the shower.

"I didn't do that to you."

for forty-five minutes

scrubbing every square inch of her body

wishing she could erase every part of herself

everything that made her her

and disappear completely

with just a washcloth and tears.


You bring out the survivor in me,

the girl who still remembers

the feeling of your fingers on her legs

and your hands on her face

Forceful;

You didn't ask.

The girl who shouted "No!"

and got you to stop for a few seconds

before starting up again,

the girl who can still feel

your lips on hers,

who thought to herself,

"There goes my first kiss,"

and still grimaces at the thought

but who can finally say

with a heavy chest

and a trembling heart,

"I am stronger now."


You bring out the survivor in me,

the winner of this battle,

the beaming glistening shining champion

with a big brass band crescendoing to her every
footstep,

and the crowd cheering her name,

no longer frightened of herself

and the person she used to be,

but instead the beautiful warrior who

because of you

now knows she can take on anything.

# The Great Cleanse

How absolutely invigorating it is to know
that only two more years must pass
until every cell in my body has been replaced
and every inch of my skin
curve of my body
strand of my hair
and thump of my heartbeat
has never been touched by you.
The venom you secreted is draining.
It's time for me to fly again.

www.ingramcontent.com/pod-product-compliance
Lightning Source LLC
Chambersburg PA
CBHW071240140726

47996CB00007B/2691